Young Heroes

Jhalak Man Tamang
Slave Labor Whistleblower

Raymond H. Miller

KIDHAVEN PRESS
An imprint of Thomson Gale, a part of The Thomson Corporation

THOMSON

™

GALE

Detroit • New York • San Francisco • New Haven, Conn. • Waterville, Maine • London

For more information, contact:
KidHaven Press
27500 Drake Rd.
Farmington Hills, MI 48331-3535
Or you can visit our Internet site at http://www.gale.com

LIBRARY OF CONGRESS CATALOGING-IN-PUBLICATION DATA

Miller, Raymond H., 1967–
    Jhalak Man Tamang : slave labor whistleblower / by Raymond H. Miller.
    p. cm. — (Young heroes)
    Includes bibliographical references and index.
    ISBN 13: 978-0-7377-3616-8 (hardcover : alk. paper)
    ISBN 10: 0-7377-3616-X (hardcover : alk. paper)
    1. Tamang, Jhalak Man. 2. Child labor—Nepal—Juvenile literature. 3. Rug and carpet industry—Nepal—Employees—Social conditions—Juvenile literature.
    4. Child labor—Law and legislation—Juvenile literature. 5. Slave labor—Juvenile literature. I. Title.
    HD6247.R942N356 2007
    331.3'18—dc22

                                                      2006018756

Contents

Chapter One

Jhalak Man Tamang

P laying with friends, eating a wholesome meal with family, going to school, and sleeping in a comfortable bed are all common activities for children in the United States and elsewhere. It is hard to believe that many children in the world today have never experienced any of these. In fact, some children spend more than twelve hours at a time in factories working under harsh conditions and receiving little or no pay. They are not allowed to leave. Jhalak Man Tamang was one of these unfortunate children.

A Tragic Tale

There is very little information about Jhalak Man Tamang's early life. He is unsure of his exact age. He was born in 1989 or 1990 somewhere in Nepal, a small country located between China and India in southern Asia. The Great Himalaya Mountain Range, which includes Mount Everest, is along Nepal's northern border. When Jhalak was a young boy, both of his parents died. With nowhere else to go, he went to live with his uncle on a farm. He helped take care of the one cow his uncle owned. It was Jhalak's job to walk the cow into the jungle to graze every day to keep the animal healthy and strong.

Jhalak enjoyed life on the farm, but he was a naturally curious boy and was eager for an education. Like a lot of other children living in rural Nepal, however, Jhalak had no opportunity to attend school. Nepal is

The rugged, green hills of Nepal's countryside are the childhood home of Jhalak Man Tamang.

Nepal

home to some of the poorest people in the world. Villages often lack the money needed to build schools.

Even in communities that have schools, many children must work rather than go to class because their families need the money they earn. They are trapped in what is known as the cycle of poverty. More than 70 percent of the people in Nepal own no land, so they cannot grow their own food. These families often work for part of the year on farms owned by others. Then they move to cities for several months to find work in industries there. They frequently do not earn enough money to pay for adequate food and shelter, so their employers encourage them to take out loans at high rates of interest. Instead of going to school, the children in these families have to work to help pay back the debt. Without an education, these children grow up to be adults who cannot obtain higher-paying jobs. The cycle continues as they too must borrow money that will take years—and, undoubtedly, the labor of their children—to pay back.

Some families are so poor that they sell their children into slavery. Other times, a stranger from the city enters a village, befriends a family, and gains their trust. Then he takes advantage of that trust, promising money and an education for a child. Most of the children, however, do not end up in school. Instead they are placed in factories.

This is what happened to Jhalak. When he was about ten years old, a family friend offered to take him to Nepal's capital city, Kathmandu. The friend promised that Jhalak could attend school while working at

Jhalak works hard on a school assignment.

the man's home. Jhalak readily accepted. However, the presumed family friend betrayed him and instead sold him to a **loom master**, someone who runs a carpet-weaving business.

"Carpet Kids"

Jhalak was just one of thousands of children working illegally in the carpet industry throughout India, Nepal, and Pakistan. They are known as the "carpet kids."

A teacher in rural Nepal instructs his students. They are among the lucky few who attend school.

Young factory workers sit at a loom weaving carpets.

Most of these children are boys. Girls are often sold to wealthy families and become servants or are put to work in other **sweatshop** industries, sewing clothes or making shoes. Carpet kids are essentially slaves of the loom master. They are never paid for the work they perform.

The conditions Jhalak faced at the factory were wretched. He was often forced to work long hours. He was sometimes at the loom from 4:00 A.M. until 11:00 P.M.—nineteen straight hours—knotting wool rugs on large, heavy wooden looms. His fingers became blistered and calloused. With no bed on which to sleep, he curled up on the dirt floor of the factory and napped whenever he could. If the owner had a large job that needed to be completed quickly, Jhalak and the other boys were made to work all night. Because their work space was dimly lit, the children had severe eyestrain from staring at the colored fiber for many hours at a time. Many carpet kids became nearsighted, which meant they could no longer clearly see faraway objects.

Perform or Be Punished

Not only were the conditions at the factory where Jhalak worked awful, the cruelty of the loom masters made the situation even worse. The children were often not allowed to leave their places at the loom to use the bathroom. If they did, they were beaten. Often they were chained to the looms to make sure they stayed put. If the loom master disapproved of a child's work, or if a child fell asleep, he was often put in a punishment room. There the child might have a rope tied around his knees and be forced to hang upside down for a long period of time. Other children had their fingers burned with hot oil. In addition to enduring beatings and torture, the carpet kids were malnourished because they were poorly fed. Without enough exercise, rest, and nutrition, the children did not grow properly.

Working at the factory did more than just affect the children physically. It also harmed their mental, social, and emotional development. They were not allowed to play with friends and they received no affection. A child **advocate** named Kailash Satyarthi described the mental

There is no playtime for this boy and many others like him, who work long hours under brutal conditions.

state of a carpet boy named Tsleem, who was about six or seven years old. He was, he said,

> benumbed to all human feelings. There was no trace of happiness or sorrow. But underneath his expressionless face I could feel the agony of his tender heart. I pulled him into my fold, caressed and cajoled him to break his silence and eventually he broke down. Once he got nostalgic, he wept thinking of his mother. This irritated the owner, and he hit Tsleem with a rod. With that [Tsleem] lost all human expression. [1]

Tsleem was later rescued.

The life that Tsleem and Jhalak led is called many things—child labor, child slavery, child work. It is real, painful, grueling, and just plain wrong. It is a reality that is much more common than many people can ever imagine.

Chapter Two

Child Labor: A Worldwide Problem

Nepal's carpet industry began in the late 1950s after China invaded Tibet. Thousands of **refugees** fled Tibet and crossed into bordering Nepal. The **United Nations** promoted carpet weaving as a source of income for those seeking shelter in Nepal from the harsh new Chinese rule. Carpet weaving had long been a part of Tibetan culture. By the 1980s, carpet had become Nepal's top **export**. Even today, many of the world' s carpets, often selling for thousands of dollars in American and European stores, come from the Kathmandu Valley in Nepal.

Carpet weaving proved to be a useful way for the Tibetans to make a living, but it also began to take on a cruel, dark side. Because children had small fingers and, usually, excellent eyesight, carpet weaving was much easier for them than for adults, and they were used more and more in the industry. By the 1970s, carpet factories were becoming filled with young children hunched over the looms, knotting and weaving. The number of child laborers in Nepal continued to rise in the 1980s and 1990s. By 1996, approximately half of Nepal's carpet weavers were children under the age of fourteen.

Brick factories like this one in Nepal often use child laborers.

Infamous Industries

Carpet weaving is not the only industry to use young children as workers. In many places throughout the world, especially in the poorest regions, many children younger than fourteen years old are forced to work illegally under abusive, hazardous, and unhealthy situations. They smash stones in quarries and make garments in clothing factories. Children as young as four years old can be found harvesting cocoa and coffee beans, fruits, sugarcane, and tea leaves. They are put to work in dangerous jobs such as **welding** in steel manufacturing businesses. Running power equipment, climbing high ladders, and working in extreme heat are among the many hazards these children face every day. Every year approximately 22,000 children die in work-related accidents.

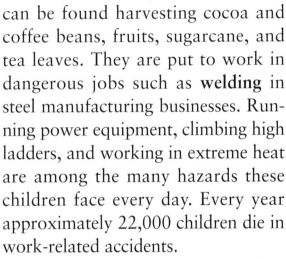

Manufacturing, especially within the **textile**, or cloth-making, industry, is one of the biggest users of child labor. A girl named Nazma Akhter was only eleven years old when she began working as a helper for sewing machine operators in Bangladesh. When she was made an operator herself, she earned about fifteen dollars a month. "I was working in the factory from eight A.M. to midnight seven days a week,"[2] she says. Nazma was beaten

Seated at their loom, four young women prepare for work on a rug.

for making mistakes or being late for work. She estimates that at least one-third of her fellow workers were younger than fourteen.

Even sports equipment, meant to bring joy and entertainment to peoples' lives, is often manufactured by children. About 80 percent of the world's soccer balls, for example, are produced in Pakistan, where child labor is common. A reporter for *Life* magazine visited a Pakistani village and wrote of his visit:

Stitching sheds are visible in every hamlet, but at each stop the masters shout at the boys to run when they see foreigners with cameras. And the ragged, barefoot kids, fearing a beating from their masters, dash into the thickets and rice fields beyond. At one compound that resembles a nest of grungy one-car garages, with no lights or ventilation, the soccer masters run shed to shed, yelling at the children to strip off the rubber finger-wraps designed to protect them from disabling thread cuts and to flee for cover.[3]

Carrying heavy bricks on their backs, two child laborers struggle up a dusty hill.

Why Children?

It is estimated that 246 million children worldwide work illegally as laborers. This is slightly less than the entire population of the United States. Almost one-third of these working children, 73 million, are younger than ten years old. Many people think that child labor exists only in undeveloped countries where poverty is commonplace. The reality is that 2.5 million of these children are located in richer areas within Europe, South America, and even North America.

There are many reasons why children are **exploited** in the workplace. Large families may need several incomes to survive and often cannot afford to send their children to school.

Akram, a child laborer from Bangladesh, is one such example. He told an interviewer about his desire to go to school. The interviewer explains,

> Akram had never been to school. He worked in a garment factory for two years before he was fired, cutting threads in the "finishing section" of the factory. He "felt bad" because other children went to school and he did not, and also described being abused by the factory managers. Akram tells me that he wanted to go to school before he started to work in the garment factory but his parents said: "We are poor, how can we send you to school?" Apparently both his mother and father wanted to enroll him in school, but could afford neither the admittance fee required by the local government primary school, nor the tutors.

Young boys break rocks that will be used for building roads in Nepal.

Instead they took him to work in a garment factory where he earned 600 taka [approximately USD $9.00] per month.[4]

In other situations, an industry lures children to work for its own profit. For example, the western African countries of Ghana and Ivory Coast produce 72 percent of the world's cocoa beans, the main ingredient in chocolate. Because buyers demand cheap beans, the growers cannot afford to pay their workers well and also make money. As a result, many growers resort to buying children, sometimes for as little as ten dollars each, to work in the field. The child slaves work long hours, spraying harmful pesticides, carrying sharp **machetes** up 25-foot (7.6m) trees, and hauling heavy bags of cocoa beans. "They are paid nothing, barely fed, and regularly beaten," writes author Mary Meinking Chambers.[5]

The use of children in abusive work environments is a worldwide problem, although in some countries it is much more common than in others. Whether the reason for it is poverty or the desire for profit, the children pay the ultimate price.

Chapter Three

Jhalak Stands His Ground

The voices of children being exploited for their labor are seldom heard. But occasionally, one child takes a stand and makes a difference. If Jhalak Man Tamang had not made a courageous decision one spring day, he and other children might have continued to be exploited in the rug factory where he worked.

On that day in April 2000, an inspector from RUGMARK, an anti–child labor program, made an unannounced visit to the factory. The inspector was there to examine the factory's working conditions. The boys at the looms were quickly ordered to get out of sight, and most of them did. Jhalak, however, stood his ground. In an act of pure bravery and determination, he did not run and hide with the other boys. Jhalak surely knew the possible results of his actions. Very few loom masters were known to be understanding or forgiving, and disobedience to a direct command usually led to swift and ruthless punishment.

21

Jhalak (left) stood up for his right to get an education and not be forced to work as a slave.

Several years earlier, a young boy in Pakistan had lost his life after speaking out against the abuse he endured in a carpet factory.

Jhalak had worked in the factory for five months—long enough to know that what was happening to him and the other boys was wrong. The inspector approached Jhalak and explained the rights he had under the child labor laws. He explained that no one at the factory could force anyone to work, and said that children, when old enough, had a right to be paid a decent wage for work they performed. He also explained that all children had a right to receive an education. He then

offered Jhalak a chance to live and go to school at a center sponsored by RUGMARK. Jhalak happily accepted the offer, left his place at the loom, and never returned.

RUGMARK to the Rescue

As Jhalak learned, RUGMARK is an organization that was created in 1994 to end illegal child labor in the rug-making industry. In the 1980s and 1990s, child advocates began to educate the public that hand-knotted carpets were being made by young children who worked as slaves. Sales of these carpets dropped greatly as a result. Worried rug manufacturers then joined with human rights groups to establish the RUGMARK labeling program.

Under the program, manufacturers agree to follow RUGMARK's strict rules against child labor. RUG-MARK inspectors make surprise visits to factories to look for any signs of children being used as workers. Rug makers who comply with the rules earn the right to place the RUGMARK label on their carpets. The labels tell buyers that the carpets were made legally, without the use of children. Having the RUGMARK label on their rugs is a way for carpet makers to in-

Children make good rug weavers because of their small, nimble fingers.

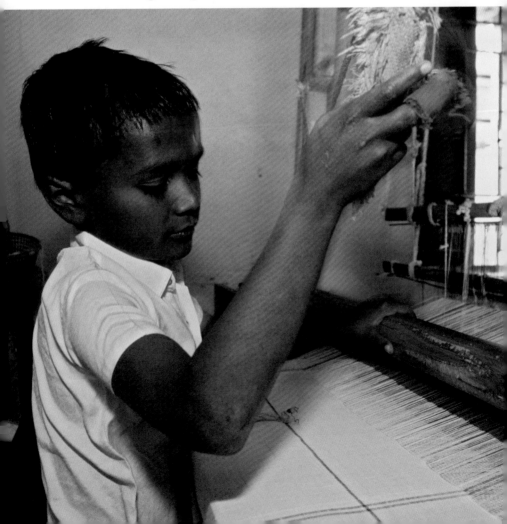

crease sales of their products, because most people do not want to buy items that are made with child labor.

The owner of the factory where Jhalak worked was not involved with RUGMARK. But he had a contract with an exporter who sold the carpets to other countries, and the exporter had recently joined the RUGMARK labeling program. Jhalak made sure the inspector knew the factory owner was not abiding by the rules.

Jhalak is not the only child that RUGMARK has aided. Between 1995 and 2004, the group rescued more than 1,500 children from carpet factories in Nepal. In

addition, the program quickly convinced numerous factory owners that using illegal child labor was just not worth the risk. Today, more than 500 manufacturers in Nepal are registered with RUGMARK.

Hamro Gar, "Our Home"

When children like Jhalak are taken out of the factories, it signals a new beginning in their young lives. "The ultimate goal is to break the cycle of poverty by moving children out of factories into schools,"[6] says Terry Collingsworth of the International Labor Rights Fund. With an education and some training, these young people can get jobs that will pay decent wages so that their children one day can go to school instead of working to pay back their parents' loans.

The RUGMARK label on a woven carpet ensures that no child labor was used.

Soon after Jhalak left the factory, he enrolled in RUGMARK's Hamro Gar school. The name Hamro Gar means "Our Home." RUGMARK sponsors several such schools in Nepal. Workers at these schools try to restore the health of former child laborers, educate them, and help them learn the skills they will need to lead a better life. Many children learn carpentry, some are taught how to make bamboo products, and others learn tailoring skills. Jhalak loved the school. He and the other children living there finally had the chance to learn and to play, two things denied them for most of their lives.

Early on at the school, Jhalak participated in a school play. The play's purpose was to teach audiences about what took place in the carpet factories. More importantly, it helped the actors cope with the memories of the abuse they endured. As Jhalak played the role of a young boy sold into the Nepalese carpet industry, he gained a clearer understanding of what had happened to him. For him, it would never happen again.

Happily Ever After?

On March 15, 2004, RUGMARK helped Jhalak get a job at a furniture shop in Nepal. It had been four years since he was freed from the carpet factory. This new workplace was entirely different from the cruel conditions at the carpet factory. According to RUGMARK, he soon began

Learning to read and write and learning a trade will benefit these boys and others like them.

leading an independent life because he was finally being paid fairly. Had he chosen to run and hide with the other children when the inspector entered the carpet-weaving factory, Jhalak most likely would have returned to his place at the loom. He might never have had a chance to

RUGMARK executive Norbert Bluem (left) and Sulochana Shresta-Shah, president of Nepal's RUGMARK Foundation, display the RUGMARK label on a Nepal made carpet.

A RUGMARK inspector reports on working conditions in an Asian carpet factory.

get an education or learn any other skills. Thanks to his courage and to RUGMARK, he received both.

Child advocacy groups such as RUGMARK are an important reason why child slavery is no longer a hidden issue. But they are only one part of the effort to make a positive difference in the lives of children who labor in unfair conditions. Individuals, governments, and independent agencies worldwide are working to end the worst child labor practices.

Chapter Four

Working to End Child Labor

The issues surrounding child labor are complex. Yet governments, human rights groups, and businesses around the world are making efforts not only to set a standard for when and how long children may be employed, but, more importantly, to bring an end to child slavery. Ordinary citizens of all ages and backgrounds are also working to make a difference in the lives of exploited children.

No Sweat

Most countries have laws to protect children from harsh working conditions, but the laws differ from country to country. Even in places where the laws are strict, they work only when the laws are enforced. One reason child slavery continues to exist in some countries is that law enforcement personnel ignore it. Because of this, a number of companies in the United States that **import** goods from other countries use labeling programs to ensure that the products they sell have not been made by children working illegally. RUGMARK is one such labeling organization.

Other industries have also adopted the use of labels. FoulBall is a label applied to soccer balls to certify that they are made without the use of child labor. When clothing companies such as Nike, L.L. Bean, or Reebok prove that their employees work in safe and healthy conditions, are paid at least the national minimum

This child from Bangladesh must work to help support his family.

wage, and are old enough to be employed, they can use a "no sweat" label. Like the RUGMARK label, the "no sweat" tag reassures the public that the items were made solely by adults.

Activism Works

One reason that Jhalak and millions of other children like him have been the victims of slavery for so many years is that until fairly recently, few people knew the extent of the problem. Organizations such as UNICEF, Child Workers in Nepal (CWIN), and others have worked hard to put child labor issues in the spotlight. As people all over the world became more aware of the realities of child slavery, changes began to happen.

Television has played a huge role in bringing about change. In 1993 NBC's *Dateline* program showed children in Bangladeshi sweatshops working to make clothing sold in Wal-Mart stores. As a result, Wal-Mart canceled its contracts with garment makers in Bangladesh. Ultimately, the Bangladeshi garment industry feared losing its profitable exports to the United States and dismissed tens of thousands of child workers.

Some critics of this method of public pressure point out that when a factory discharges the children working there, only half of the problem is addressed. Because their families still need them to bring in money, these children may end up in even worse circumstances. They sometimes go to work in secret shops in more dreadful conditions than before or take more hazardous jobs such as stone crushing and brick making.

Chinese workers make sports bags for Nike in a factory that was once a sweatshop.

Workers in China make DVDs that will be sold by Wal-Mart and other stores.

To make a lasting change, it takes the involvement of everyone—labeling programs, governments, and activists—to make a difference. Otherwise, the temporary gains may result only in bigger setbacks. Even individual citizens play a role in helping to solve a tough problem.

Decisions, Decisions

Is it possible to make responsible decisions with all of the issues surrounding the use of forced child labor in some parts of the world? Should people refuse to buy a pair of brand-name sneakers or jeans, orange juice, sporting equipment, or a rug if it is possible that exploited child workers made them? What if products that are guaranteed to be child-labor free cost more? Will one person's buying habits even make a difference globally? There are no easy answers to these questions, which are being raised as new insights are gained about child labor in the world market.

Surveys have shown that a majority of people would be willing to pay slightly more for the guarantee that an item of clothing was not made in a sweatshop employing children. The difficulty lies in the fact that it is not

East Indian children take part in a demonstration urging people to boycott products made by child labor.

always possible to know whether an item is child-labor free. Some products may have a label saying that they are not made with the use of child labor, but the absence of a label does not necessarily mean that a product was made by children. Some industries simply do not use a labeling program. So, a little investigation is necessary. The U.S. Department of Labor, Co-Op America, Corporate Watch, UNITE, and the National Consumers League all maintain lists of companies that have pledged not to do business with sweatshops.

The fact that products sold in the United States may have been made by young children has outraged many people enough to **boycott,** or stop buying, specific products, such as certain brands of clothing, sports equipment, and carpets. Companies faced with unhappy customers will usually change their methods of doing business. A few determined individuals go a step further by actively campaigning for change.

Joining a Campaign

Thousands of young people have taken part in campaigns against child labor. In 1995, when Craig Kielburger of Thornhill, Ontario, was twelve years old, he read about the life of a boy named Iqbal Masih. Iqbal was an enslaved carpet weaver in Pakistan who escaped and helped free other children.

Kielburger wanted to do something himself. He began speaking about child labor at his school and later formed a group called Free the Children. At the invitation of the International Program on the Elimination of Child Labor (IPEC), the young Canadian traveled to

Young Canadian activist Craig Kielburger addresses students about child labor.

Bangladesh, India, Nepal, Pakistan, and Thailand to personally observe child labor conditions. Kielburger visited factories, met child laborers, and even did some of the work expected of children his age.

Kielburger then began his own letter-writing campaign, which inspired many other students in schools across Canada and the United States. Many of these students decided to raise funds for a number of organizations and for a school that Iqbal wanted to build in his village for other children freed from forced labor. That school opened in 1996.

As Kielburger discovered, letter writing is an effective tool. Concerned people can write to manufacturers to find out whether they use child labor, or to embassies in the United States to learn more from ambassadors of various countries about how their nations protect children. Contacting members of Congress by phone, fax, or mail is an excellent way to receive more information about efforts to stem global child labor as well as to express a viewpoint.

Campaigns such as the Global March Against Child Labour are another avenue for involvement. The Global March was started in 1998 by Kailash Satyarthi, who gave up his career to help children being used as slaves in Indian businesses.

President Fernando Cardoso of Brazil greets young members of the Global March Against Child Labour.

Many changes have been made in the effort to stop child labor, and the story of Jhalak Man Tamang shows that those changes have made a difference. Jhalak risked his life to take a stand, and the involvement of organizations such as RUGMARK provided him a way out of the carpet factory. But for the 246 million children still experiencing the daily horrors of forced labor, the battle continues.

Notes

Chapter One: Jhalak Man Tamang

1. Kailash Satyarthi, *Break the Chains, Save the Childhood*. New Delhi: South Asian Coalition on Child Servitude, 1997.

Chapter Two: Child Labor: A Worldwide Problem

2. Quoted in *Multinational Monitor*, "A Former Child Laborer's Shopfloor View: An Interview with Nazma Akhter," January/February 1997.
3. Sydney H. Schanberg and Jimmie Briggs, "Six Cents an Hour," *Life*, June 1996, p. 39.
4. Quoted in Burns H. Weston, ed., *Child Labor and Human Rights: Making Children Matter*. Boulder, CO: Lynne Rienner, 2005, p. 32.
5. Mary Meinking Chambers, "Chocolate-Coated Slavery," *Faces*, April 2006, p. 32.

Chapter Three: Jhalak Stands His Ground

6. Quoted in Suzanne Charles, "Children of the Looms," Ford Foundation, Spring 2001. www.fordfound.org/publications/ ff_report/view_ff_report_detail.cfm? report_index=287.

Glossary

advocate: A person who argues for, recommends, or supports a person, cause, or policy.

boycott: To protest by avoiding dealings with a business or organization.

exploited: Taken advantage of.

export: To send items to another country for trade or sale.

import: To brings items in from a foreign country in order to sell them.

loom master: Someone who supervises those who work at a weaving loom in a carpet factory.

machete: Large, heavy knives used for cutting sugarcane and underbrush and as weapons.

refugees: People who flee from one place to another to take refuge from war, disaster, or political reasons.

sweatshop: A shop or factory where employees work long hours for low pay in poor conditions.

textile: Cloth or fabric.

United Nations: An international organization founded in 1945 to promote peace, security, and development throughout the world.

welding: Joining metals by applying heat and sometimes pressure.

For Further Exploration

Books

Francesco D'Adamo, *Iqbal.* Translated by Ann
Lenori. New York: Atheneum, 2003. Based on
the true story of a Pakistani boy determined to
free himself and other children from their
bondage in the carpet factories.

Shirlee P. Newman, *Child Slavery in Modern
Times.* New York: Franklin Watts, 2000. An
eye-opening book showing how children are
forced to work long hours in factories, fields,
and private homes all over the world.

Cathryne L. Schmitz, Elizabeth KimJin Traver,
and Desi Larson, *Child Labor: A Global
View.* Westport, CT: Greenwood, 2004. A
look at the contributing factors of child
labor in fifteen specific countries, with
details of the conditions, the history of the
problem, political policies, and the outlook
for the future.

Jane Wilsher, *Stand Up, Speak Out.*
Minneapolis: Two-Can Publishing, 2002.
Ideas, paintings, poems, and stories written
by young people from around the world on
the topic of children's rights.

Web sites

Global March Against Child Labour (www.global
march.org/). Easy-to-read information about
the annual Global March Against Child
Labour and current efforts underway to make
changes around the world.

RUGMARK Foundation (www.rugmark.org/).
The RUGMARK Foundation's Web site tells
how to purchase carpets with the RUGMARK
label and provides a wealth of facts and
information about child labor in the carpet
industry, including news and current events.

Index

Picture Credits

About the Author

Raymond H. Miller is the author of more than fifty nonfiction books for children. He has written on a range of topics from U.S. presidents to American Indians. He enjoys playing sports and spending time outdoors with his wife and three children.